40 DAYS WITH THE SAVIOR

CONNIE E. SOKOL

PRAISE FOR 40 DAYS WITH THE SAVIOR

"Connie Sokol, the queen of simple yet effective, has done it again. What a great resource for quick, daily things that we can do to draw closer to the Savior. This easily fits into our busy lives, reminding us of what matters most."

—Peggy Urry, President-elect, American Night Writers Association

"I LOVED this book! Connie brings these scriptures home with real, everyday moments. I can savor these bite-size gems throughout my busy day with little ones. The teachings are powerful, and her added insights brought them home for me in a new way."

—Amy Chandler, Founder, My Story Matters

"Connie Sokol's new book, "40 Days with the Savior", is just the little push I needed to feel the Savior's presence in my daily life. Using personal stories, scriptural accounts, and meaningful insights, she helps readers draws closer to Jesus Christ and become a more Christ-centered person. I loved her daily nuggets of wisdom, with titles like, "He Did the Right Thing" and "He Gently Corrects", to prompt a change of behavior. My Easter will be more meaningful this year!"

—Jodi Marie Robinson, Author of "Women of Virtue" and "A Royal Guardian"

"Connie Sokol has thoughtfully shared fresh insights to well know scriptural phrases. The simple meditations in **40 Days with the Savior** are enlightening and empowering. This is an easy way to draw closer to Jesus Christ throughout the Easter season and during the rest of the year. After reading this book I feel my burdens are lighter."

—Margaret Turley, Author of Save the Child, Administrator Writers Unite to Fight Cancer

40 Days with the Savior

VYNE PUBLISHING

WOODLAND HILLS, UT

ISBN: 978-0-9890196-0-6

Published by Vyne Publishing, 865 S. Oak Dr., Woodland Hills, UT 84653

Second printing.

Cover design by Kelli Ann Morgan
Cover design © 2012 by Connie E. Sokol

INTRODUCTION

Originally, the idea for *40 Days with the Savior* came from wanting a more Christ-centered Christmas.

During the month of December, I posted on my website a daily scripture and thought on a character trait of the Savior. Due to requests, I created the book *24 Days with the Savior* and donated all proceeds to local food banks.

The experience changed my entire Christmas season. Reading daily posts about the Savior helped me feel and be noticeably kinder, happier, and more peaceful.

At a friend's suggestion, I created this book to have a more Christ-centered Easter in the same way. Before beginning His ministry, the Savior spiritually prepared for forty days in the wilderness. I named this book *40 Days with the Savior* as a reminder that we can also become more spiritually prepared for what lies ahead. And as with my other book, all proceeds are donated to charity.

If you're looking for a simple but powerful way to know the Savior better, and perhaps become more like Him (albeit a small step at a time), these forty daily scriptures and devotionals about His character traits can help in a surprising way.

I can attest from personal experience.

Last Christmas season, I was busily preparing our big family for a big trip. At the same time, I was finishing the last chapters of the *24 Days with the Savior*. With so many demands and tasks, proper timing and sequencing became crucial. One morning, I readied my daily blog post on the Savior, then hurried to leave with my baby for errands and a desperately needed hair appointment. Timing was right down to the minute, but I could make it, when suddenly, my car keys were gone. Even after searching the usual places, they couldn't be found. My baby cried, time ticked, and my frustration mounted.

Then the thought came—my husband had the keys last.

I groaned aloud. *Not again*, I muttered. *Each time he takes my car, I end up on a key search the next morning.* After fifteen minutes and my unanswered phone calls to said hubby, I located the keys. Speeding down the road, thoroughly late, and with no loving feelings for my husband, I picked up my cell phone to remind him to leave the keys on my desk next time.

A thought came to me, crystal clear—"patience."

I started to smile, then chuckle. Because you see, my Savior blog post THAT VERY MORNING had been on Jesus' patience. At that moment in the car, I remembered that I'd written about how loving and tolerant He was with our childlike and annoying ways. Suddenly, lost keys didn't constitute a federal offense or upsetting my husband, and I put down the phone.

That one blog post saved my husband stress and our marriage a negative hit. And it helped me see the selfishness in my mindset.

I hope that as you read these daily devotionals, you too will have these kinds of life-changing moments. The kind that help you remember the Savior, and then truly, really, want to be more to be like Him. The kind that keep the reason for each special season or daily desire to connect forefront in your heart and soul.

Partial proceeds from this book purchase go to wonderful causes to help families. I hope you will read more about these causes and share your experiences using this book with me at www.conniesokol.com.

DEDICATION

To my loving, spiritually-grounded family,
faithful friends, and numerous good people
who motivate me to be a little bit better every single day.
And to my Savior, whom I love,
and who continually brings me joy, growth, and peace.

TABLE OF CONTENTS

DAY 1: HE PREPARED SPIRITUALLY FOR THE DAY

Matthew 5:1
And seeing the multitudes, he went up into a mountain: and when he was set, his disciples came unto him.

I think of this scripture often. I don't have multitudes coming at me daily, but I have seven children, which feels like a multitude. And I don't have disciples that come to me, but I have family, friends, neighbors, and people I meet who daily need to be loved, cheered, and encouraged. Instead of hurrying out of bed and going through a lengthy to-do list, Jesus went to a quiet place, talked with His Heavenly Father, and prepared spiritually for whatever difficulties were sure to come.

That's a good idea.

Constantly caring for others brings joy, peace, and fulfillment. But it can also drain our reserves. Especially as mothers, we can get "set" for the day as the Savior did and receive that spiritual boost and perspective we will need to get through it. Accessing His peace and love allows us to more fully enjoy serving and caring, as well as feel a greater connection to the ultimate Caregiver.

What one thing you can do to spiritually prepare for the day?

DAY 2: HE KNEW HIS DIVINE ROLE

John 8:12

Then spake Jesus again unto them, saying, I am the light of the world: he that followeth me shall not walk in darkness, but shall have the light of life.

The Savior is known by many names that are often related to the roles He fulfills: Savior, Redeemer, Mediator, Light of the World, the Good Shepherd, and many more. Wonderfully, He fulfills those roles, in various ways, without confusion or frustration.

It seems to me that Jesus knew who He was and what He was to do as the Son of God: take on a mortal body, atone for the sins of man that we might have eternal life, and be resurrected to give all the gift of immortality.

That's clarity.

One January, I considered my different life roles: woman, wife, mother, friend, neighbor, author, speaker, Sunday School teacher, and more. Instead of allowing myself to feel overwhelmed by the number of hats I needed to wear, I chose a *few* roles and *one* thing I could improve about each of them. Then I happily focused on making small changes during the year.

As a woman, I focused on listening more and talking less (with my family's complete support). As a wife, I created more day-to-day fun with my husband (big events and stolen moments). And as a mother, I worked on helping my children develop their talents (piano practice ad nauseum).

I didn't improve these roles perfectly. But keeping a clear vision of who I was and how I could better fulfill my responsibilities led to small changes that yielded big results.

The Savior's example of knowing and fulfilling His roles teaches us that knowing our identity as a beloved child of God leads us to better understand and accomplish that role and the many others related to it.

What is one thing I can do today to better fulfill and enjoy one of my roles?

DAY 3: HE FULFILLED HIS PURPOSE

Matthew 4:2–3, 10–11

And when he had fasted forty days and forty nights, he was afterward an hungered. And when the tempter came to him . . .

Then saith Jesus unto him, Get thee hence, Satan: for it is written, Thou shalt worship the Lord thy God, and him only shalt thou serve. Then the devil leaveth him.

Jesus was tempted by Satan to turn stones into bread, to throw Himself down from a high place so angels could rescue Him and, finally, with the supposed riches of the world if He would worship Satan.

Food, fame, and fortune. That's basically what it came down to for the Savior, and what it comes down to for us. And though Jesus was presented with these temptations, He remained true to His purpose in fulfilling His divine destiny as the Savior of mankind.

Throughout our lives, we'll have similar temptations that threaten to pull us from our true focus. Today, women particularly have so many options and talents that it's easy to get distracted from what we are meant to be: mothers who nurture and women who serve with purpose as we strive to follow the Savior. As author Sheri Dew once said, we tend to focus on our wardrobes, waistlines, and bank accounts, and for what? Those distractions will take us on roads and in directions that won't lead to lasting happiness.

I recently spoke with a friend about this very thing. We had both reread "Of Regrets and Resolutions" by President Dieter F. Uchtdorf, a life-changing talk on so many levels. This good woman shared that after reading it she had evaluated her busy life. As a mother, photographer, graphic designer, and more, she was also an author with a book to be completed and released in a few weeks. However, after considering the talk's principles, she chose to postpone the book release and spend more time with her family. This choice likely disappointed some but definitely blessed those who mattered most.

These kinds of fork-in-the-road decisions may seem small, but they are pivotal. Each time we choose to stay focused on our true purpose, refusing to be tempted by the lure of physical appetite, wealth, or self-importance, we find greater peace, fulfillment, and joy in who we are truly meant to become.

What is my most important purpose right now and how can I better focus on it?

DAY 4: HE DIDN'T SEEK OTHERS' APPROVAL

Mark 2:14–16

And as he passed by, he saw Levi [Matthew] the son of Alphaeus sitting at the receipt of custom, and said unto him, Follow me. And he arose and followed him.

And it came to pass, that, as Jesus sat at meat in his house, many publicans and sinners sat also together with Jesus and his disciples: for there were many, and they followed him.

And when the scribes and Pharisees saw him eat with publicans and sinners, they said unto his disciples, How is it that he eateth and drinketh with publicans and sinners?

Throughout His ministry, the Savior continued to balk superficial religious traditions and prejudices by behaving honestly. He saw into people's hearts. And good people responded in kind.

Matthew was a tax gatherer in Capernaum, a profession universally disliked by the Jewish people because of the corrupt Roman tax system. And yet because Jesus knew Matthew's heart, knew he was a good and honest man, the Savior refused to cave to social pressures and called him to be one of His chosen disciples. And Matthew accepted, despite the reactions of others.

Too often, we spend our precious time and energy worrying about what others think.

My daughter taught me something about this. Once, when a family came to visit us, everyone headed for the family room, but the mother entered the living room to sit down for a moment. My seven-year-old daughter went over to her and in her childlike honesty said, "We don't usually sit in here. It's just the look room."

Jesus didn't have any "look rooms." He made no pretense at appearances, nor did He worry what others thought about his lodgings, clothing, financial situation, educational background, or work status. The Savior focused on teaching doctrine, lifting others, and performing miracles.

How often do you and I worry about the opinions of others—a nosy neighbor, a competitive coworker, or an over-the-top parent volunteer working with us in the classroom? Most of our stress comes from looking laterally instead of vertically. When we look *up* to the Savior and our Heavenly Father for our true identity, we find who we are in the peace and clarity of truth, instead of losing ourselves in the chaotic messages of society.

How can you focus on the Savior and not on others' approval today?

DAY 5: HE SHUNNED ADULATION

John 12:12–13

On the next day much people that were come to the feast, when they heart that Jesus was coming to Jerusalem, took branches of palm trees, and went forth to meet him, and cried, Hosanna: Blessed is the King of Israel that cometh in the name of the Lord.

I'm amazed by the Savior's constant ability to keep perspective even as multitudes thronged, adored, and celebrated Him. He understands what happens when we become too aware of our own good and focus on others' compliments.

In the scripture above, the people crowded the streets leading to the temple, shouting praises to Him as their Lord. Within one week, these same multitudes would shout again, only this time calling for His crucifixion.

Jesus knew that this adulation was fleeting. And on a hillside filled with thousands of adoring people, He unhesitatingly taught the real doctrines and hard truths that would ultimately bring them happiness. He taught knowing they wouldn't like the here and now of that doctrine and that many would walk away, unable to continue with Him because it was just too hard to hear.

I'm grateful for His example, for the way He constantly showed that praise from society, or lack of, means nothing.

8

Whether people praise you or not really doesn't matter in the end. Whether you're an unappreciated mother, an overlooked office worker, or an unpaid volunteer, feel the value of what you do within yourself. The important things are to be true to what you know is right; to love, work and serve to the best of your ability; and put first that which matters most.

How can I feel valued even if I'm not being praised or complimented?

DAY 6: HE SUBMITTED

Matthew 26:39
And he went a little further, and fell on his face, and prayed, saying, O my Father, if it be possible, let this cup pass from me: nevertheless not as I will, but as thou wilt.

To me, this is one of the most poignant passages in all of scripture. This wonderful, righteous, dutiful Son had a terrible commission to fulfill. He wanted to obey the Father but was aware on a certain level of how excruciating this sacrifice might be. And yet He said, "Nevertheless . . ." and moved on to accomplish the greatest, most selfless act in history.

I'm so grateful that He allowed us see into this deeply private moment—that even He, the Son of God, the most obedient and willing person to ever live, did not want to do this thing.

But He did.

As I look back on my life, it seems that the most pivotal, most life-changing experiences were the times that I finally submitted to what was right: changing my lifelong dream of broadcasting to a teaching major; homeschooling my Asperger's son; having a baby at forty-six. These and other decisions didn't look particularly appealing at the time; some even made me feel downright defiant. And yet it was taking that sometimes awful first step—the opening of the soul in faith—that led to later and much greater blessings and joy.

I have come to feel that something isn't deep submission unless, however right the thing before you is, a part of you really, truly doesn't want to do it.

And yet you do it anyway.

I read an excerpt from Arthur Miller's play, *After the Fall*, where one of the characters says: "I tried to die near the end of the war. The same dream returned to me each night. . . . I dreamed I had a child. And even in the dream I felt that the child was my life, and it was an idiot, and I ran away from it . . . until I thought, if I could kiss it, whatever was in it that was my own, perhaps I could sleep again. And I bent to its broken face, and it was horrible. But I kissed it. I think, Quentin, one must finally take one's life into one's own arms, and kiss it." (Leo Buscaglia, *Living, Loving, Learning,* New York: Ballantine Books, 1982, 78).

In each of our lives there are choices, situations, or experiences to which we will need to submit, whether through acceptance, change, or faith. But in the submitting, we'll find the greater good and more lasting joy that we ultimately seek.

How can you better submit to something that is right but that feels too difficult?

DAY 7: HE BORE BEING MISUNDERSTOOD

Matthew 13:55-57

Is not this the carpenter's son? is not his mother called Mary? and his brethren, James, and Joses, and Simon, and Judas? And his sisters, are they not all with us? Whence then hath this man all these things?

And they were offended in him. But Jesus said unto them, A prophet is not without honour, save in his own country, and in his own house.

Sometimes, even with our best intentions, our actions or words can be misunderstood. Or maligned. Or wrongly judged. The word that stands out to me in this scripture is *offended*.

We see the Savior serving, loving, healing, and going about doing good. And still, when He claimed his rightful divine title, the people were upset and felt He thought He was better than they were. Even when His actions clearly showed the pure purpose and desire of His heart, the people refused to see that truth and instead chose to be offended.

Some were even unhappy that Jesus was doing good *and succeeding*. In Matt 21:15, it says, "And when the chief priests and scribes saw the wonderful things that he did . . . they were sore displeased."

Have you felt misunderstood? Or that you've tried so hard to do something right only to have it turn out so very wrong? Or to find that people disliked you for doing good?

Don't worry. Go forward. Ignore the naysayers, armchair coaches, and sideline gossipers. Throughout your life, you can count on some judging you unfairly, whether unintentionally or intentionally. Move on with your life and keep doing good. Ultimately, these negative people or experiences will drop from your life, like chaff from wheat, and you will be left with loyal friends and sweet experiences.

How can you move forward without taking offense today?

DAY 8: HE SACRIFICED FOR OTHERS

Luke 22:42, 44

[He said], Father, if thou be willing, remove this cup from me: nevertheless not my will, but thine be done. And being in an agony he prayed more earnestly: and his sweat was as it were great drops of blood falling down to the ground.

In a way incomprehensible to us, the Savior suffered the sins of everyone who has ever lived. But even more amazing, He could have chosen to vicariously feel our pains from a distance and remain only a kind friend or compassionate neighbor. Instead, He actually felt our same feelings, experienced our same pains, and walked our same path. This perfectly pure and clean Son of God *chose* to completely get down on our level.

Why?

So he could best know how to succor us. So He could know fully and completely know how to take away the pain.

The Savior sacrificed everything—His personal desires, His comforts, even His will—so that we might have ultimate happiness. He gave us the possibility of a clean slate after each mistake, to let it go and be better next time. He loves us fully and completely, no matter our spiritual state, and only wants us to be happy and to be like Him.

14

Jesus teaches us a core principle: sacrifice is a gift of joy.

He suffered so that we don't have to. When we're sad, angry, or overwhelmed with the wrongness of our choices, we don't have to stay that way. He already bore those burdens. And because of this, we can be happier. As we meet others, we can pay it forward and follow His example by sacrificing our time and abilities to share others' burdens and lighten their load.

How can you sacrifice for someone today?

15

DAY 9: HE TURNED FROM MATERIALISM

Matthew 8:20

And Jesus saith unto him, The foxes have holes, and the birds of the air have nests; but the Son of man hath not where to lay his head.

A quick look at today's top-selling books and magazines shows titles and headlines on how to make more money, be well-liked, and live a glamorous life.

One literary agent shared in her blog that she used to read these kinds of magazines. But after a time she felt unhappy and unfulfilled. Thinking through her life, she realized her feelings stemmed from reading about false images and fake lives. She tossed the magazines and her happiness increased.

More money, bigger homes, fancier cars. These mean nothing to the Savior. He knows the obvious truth that too many easily forget: we can't take it with us. The constant focus on more keeps us distracted from true priorities in our lives. Instead of living generously, we focus on acquiring things. Instead of helping the needy, we believe the myth that more will make us happier.

It won't.

Research shows that lottery winners have a level of happiness either equal to or less than before they received their winnings. More money means more stewardship, more stress, more decisions, and more taxes.

The Savior avoided stress and temptation by knowing what He truly needed and who it ultimately came from. And then He instructed His Apostles to do the same, going neither by purse nor scrip. Even in the Lord's Prayer, the Savior asks the Father to give us this day our *daily* bread.

We can do the something similar: offer a simple prayer of gratitude, actively look for ways to serve, or spend quality time with those we love. As we are present in the moment, we experience the truly priceless.

How can you let go of focusing on material things and instead see someone's present need?

DAY 10: HE DID THE RIGHT THING

Luke 10:30–34

And by chance there came down a certain priest that way: and when he saw him, he passed by on the other side. And likewise a Levite, when he was at the place, came and looked on him, and passed by on the other side.

But a certain Samaritan, as he journeyed, came where he was: and when he saw him, he had compassion on him, and went to him, and bound up his wounds, pouring in oil and wine, and set him on his own beast, and brought him to an inn, and took care of him.

This parable becomes more meaningful when we realize that in Jesus' time the Jews hated the Samaritans for apostatizing from the Israelite religion. Negative feelings ran so deep for the Samaritans that to get to Jerusalem, Jews would walk *around* Samaria—about an extra day's walk—rather than use the shorter, more direct route through it.

For Jesus to tell the Jewish people not only to acknowledge these supposedly heathen people, but then depict a Samaritan as the hero of the story and expose the hypocrisy of a priest was beyond appalling.

It didn't matter. Nor did it matter that what Jesus said made them angry. Or that it offended their personal beliefs or traditions. Or that they might try to hurt Him for speaking the truth. Jesus stood firm against the cultural traditions of the day. He did the right thing and let people respond as they may.

Certainly the parable of the good Samaritan teaches us the importance of helping the downtrodden, but I believe there's so much more to it. It teaches us that we're to overcome our judgmental tendencies and respond to a need before us, no matter how distasteful, inconvenient, or contradictory to societal or cultural norms.

One man serving in a church capacity in Africa said he was headed to a church meeting when he saw a young boy crying hysterically on the side of the road. His first thought was to help the child, but he realized, "I can't be late to the meeting as I'm the presiding authority." Arriving at the church, he gave his car keys to another church member, told him of the situation, and asked him to bring the boy to the church. After that was done, they discovered the boy had lost his earnings selling fish that day. If he returned to his caregiver without the money, he would be beaten or cast out. They comforted him, restored his losses, and took him back to his caregiver.

Being a good Samaritan can be a simple thing. It can mean seeing another's need in everyday life—no matter whose need it is—and responding appropriately to it. It can be refraining from judging another unfairly, but giving that person the benefit of the doubt. And it can be treating a neighbor with love and kindness, the very things we hope to receive.

How can you be more open and responsive to those you meet today?

19

DAY 11: HE INFLUENCED OTHERS FOR GOOD

John 6:67-68
Then said Jesus unto the twelve, Will ye also go away?
Then Simon Peter answered him, Lord, to whom shall we go?
Thou hast the words of eternal life.

Peter chose to follow the Savior because He taught and lived truth. And that truth had dramatically influenced this disciple's life for good. Peter had become a new man through Christ's intensely personal tutoring.

Consider the people you've met over the years—who has influenced your life for good? A teacher, a coach, a neighbor?

My sixth-grade teacher, Miss Lynda Hatch, forever impacted my life through her dedicated teaching and personal encouragement. During a difficult time for me personally, Miss Hatch recognized my need to feel valued. At school I was chosen as a special helper, given important responsibilities, and encouraged to be my best self. Occasionally after school, she would invite me and another student to help grade papers. When I wrote a poem for our class competition, she expressed her admiration and ultimately showed it to the principal, who wrote a complimentary note about the quality of writing.

Because of her warmth, direct manner, and extra attention, my self-confidence flourished and my writing improved. And because of her powerful and positive influence, I obtained a teaching degree and then became a published author.

One young man on a baseball team showed himself to be different than others. He chose not to swear, drink, or engage in behaviors unbecoming to a young man his age. Throughout the season, his baseball coach watched the consistent choices of this young man. The coach eventually changed his own personal habits to live a happier, more value-based life because of the young player's excellent example.

We each have the opportunity to be that kind of example to others, including our families. We can look for those opportunities to influence. And though they may seem small, even inconsequential, we can intuitively know where to place our energy and effort to make that influence felt.

The Savior positively influences us because His love, goodness, and actions are consistent with His teachings. When we love others and try to live as best as we believe, our influence becomes a powerful tool for good, too.

Who can I more positively influence today?

DAY 12: HE GAVE UP PERSONAL COMFORTS

Matthew 6:25, 28, 31, 34

Consider the lilies of the field, how they grow; they toil not, neither do they spin. Therefore take no thought, saying, What shall we eat? Or, What shall we drink? Or, Wherewithal shall we be clothed?

Take therefore no thought for the morrow: for the morrow shall take thought for the things of itself. Sufficient unto the day is the evil thereof.

As a mother, I feel that I give up personal comforts on a daily basis. And I'm not always that happy about it. Just when I sit down to rest, someone needs a ride. Or when I believe the laundry is finally done, my sons bring their previously hidden and overflowing baskets to the laundry room. Even in typing these devotionals on the Savior, I continually make the goal to rise early to complete them, and without fail, my baby keeps me up all night.

And I am not alone. One of my friends, a mother of nine, said she had finished all she needed to do one evening and was finally squeezing in a much-needed soak in the tub. At an opportune moment, she ran the warm water in the bath and added her favorite but rarely used lavender salts. However, her children needed eleventh-hour help with their schoolwork, and so, with one last longing look, she drained the tub.

These seem like small things, but they don't feel that small. And though it's nothing compared to what the Savior gave, I believe most of us feel the frustration of these lesser sacrifices even more than the larger ones.

Ultimately, the more obvious the sacrifice, the easier it might be to make. One year we planned to take our children to Disneyland but heard about a needy family in the neighborhood. When we approached our children about using the vacation money to help the family, without hesitation, they said, "Sure." I think most children would respond similarly.

The harder sacrifices, then, are those needling interruptions, relentless demands, and continual last-minute saves. And yet the very constancy of this opposition creates an opportunity for us to develop softness, humility, and patience. With those traits, the Savior can work with our spirits, changing our hearts and minds for the better.

Daily frustrations of life do provide a purpose. And as we give up watching our favorite TV show to read to a child, or miss an exercise class to visit a struggling friend, we actually gain more spiritual comfort than we had expected.

What personal comforts can you give up today to love someone else more immediately and fully?

DAY 13: HE SPENT TIME APART

Matthew 4:1–2
Then was Jesus led up of the Spirit into the wilderness . . . and when he had fasted forty days and forty nights . . .
Mark 1:35
And in the morning, rising up a great while before day, he went out, and departed into a solitary place, and there prayed.

Jesus Christ knew the importance of taking time to get spiritually grounded. Before He began his three-year ministry, Jesus took this time to commune with His Heavenly Father and gain spiritual strength for what needed to be done.

How often do we roll out of bed in the morning, grumble at the day, hurry to dress and drive ourselves to the workplace or our children to school, never thinking about the energy and rejuvenation we could experience by making a simple course correction.

What if this morning, you begin by reading one of these daily devotionals? Or say a brief prayer of gratitude, along with a request for health and guidance? How would that change your choices? Your mindset? Your experiences throughout the day?

When I don't pray or read scripture, I can tell you what I do experience: small annoyances, forgetful episodes, and frequent frustrations. I continually feel out of alignment with the day. I get more bad news and flat tires. I feel less inclined to serve and more self-focused. All that from one simple choice?

Absolutely.

What is one spiritually-grounding choice I can make today?

DAY 14: HE IS CHEERFUL

John 16:33

These things I have spoken unto you, that in me ye might have peace. In the world ye shall have tribulation: but be of good cheer; I have overcome the world.

I love the positive nature of the Savior! Even when He daily dealt with plagues and sicknesses among the multitudes, corruption and vindictiveness from the Pharisees, and the bitter and overwhelming knowledge of His future horrors, still, He was cheerful.

Some days, I'm just not that cheerful. And yet as I was recently talking with a friend, whining about something in my life that wasn't happening as fast as I would like it to, I stopped talking. Then I said, "You know, if that's the worst my life has to offer, then things are great."

Maybe you are experiencing financial stress, emotional difficulties, or just plain exhaustion. Maybe the water heater goes out, the car breaks down, or your child is in trouble at school. Again. Or maybe you're facing the serious trial of divorce, the loss of a loved one, or terminal illness.

Whatever the challenge or trial, know that He has borne not only your sins but your fears, sorrows, and heartaches. And done so for billions and billions of people, just so that we all, very personally, might have joy. That we might have peace. That we might have cheer. He has overcome the world

26

so that we can be happier today.

How can you be more cheerful in your conversation or actions today?

DAY 15: HE IS A FRIEND

John 15:13

Greater love hath no man than this, that a man lay down his life for his friends. Ye are my friends, if ye do whatsoever I command you.

One of my favorite stories in the Bible is when the palsied man is carried to the Savior by his four friends. The four men carrying the litter (a stretcher) were kept from getting inside the house and to the Savior because of the multitude.

But instead of giving up or saying, "Sorry, buddy, we just couldn't get in," they got creative. Hook or by crook—or by tile—they were going to help their friend be healed. With great faith, the friends carried the litter and carefully negotiated the narrow stairs on the side of the house to the rooftop. Here, they found the roof opening too small.

What to do?

Make it bigger, of course. With moxie and determination, these friends began ripping off roof tiles to enlarge the opening. I can only imagine Jesus gently smiling or even chuckling softly as they lowered the litter down to where the He stood. And then He healed the man, who went out rejoicing with his devoted friends.

That's the kind of friend the Savior is to us. He is always there, always helping, always working on our behalf and never giving up on us. Do we remember that? In times of loneliness or misunderstanding, do we truly remember that we have a constant friend and companion who can help us feel peace, contentment, truth, and comfort? We only have to "pray to the Father" to ask for it, and we can receive the companionship of the Holy Ghost to feel it.

So if people or life or situations make you feel friendless, remember, you always have a friend in Him.

How can you be a more devoted friend today?

DAY 16: HE IS MERCIFUL

Luke 13:10-13

And he was teaching in one of the synagogues on the Sabbath. And, behold, there was a woman which had a spirit of infirmity eighteen years, and was bowed together, and could in no wise lift up herself.

And when Jesus saw her, he called her to him, and said unto her, Woman, thou art loosed from thine infirmity. And he laid his hands on her: and immediately she was made straight, and glorified God.

Some think of Deity as being unkind, emotionless, or even punishing. But when we read the scriptures, we find God and Jesus Christ to be loving, compassionate, and always merciful, giving us the most possible good in any situation. This poor crippled woman had lived in a physically deformed state for many years, unable to even lift herself to stand upright. And along comes the Savior, mercifully aware of her and able to heal the infirmity.

In our daily lives, we experience more peace and true happiness when we extend mercy, especially when we're justified in not doing so.

Years ago I read about a woman, Victoria Ruvolo, whose life was changed forever by a senseless act of violence. A teenager had thrown a twenty-pound frozen turkey from his speeding vehicle into the windshield of the car Victoria was driving. Afterward, she required six hours of surgery, the surgeons piecing her face together using metal plates. Victoria could have retaliated, or would have been justified in seeking the highest penalty. But this good woman insisted on offering the teenager a plea deal, sparing him a possible sentence of twenty-five years in prison. She changed this young man's life forever with a careful, merciful choice.

In the courtroom, the young man made his way to Victoria and tearfully apologized. She stood, embraced the weeping boy, stroked his head, and said, "It's okay. I just want you to make your life the best it can be." (For the full account, see "Forgiveness Has Power to Change Future," *Deseret Morning News*, Aug. 21, 2005, p. AA3.)

The next time justice is in our hands, hopefully we can gently and lovingly wield it, knowing we'll be on the receiving end all too soon.

How can you be more merciful to someone today?

DAY 17: HE IS PATIENT

Repeatedly in the scriptures we see the Savior's patience—with His disciples, with the multitudes, with the Pharisees. He patiently taught gospel truths despite the people's difficulty in processing them. He patiently showed civic duty by paying taxes, though He was the Son of God. And He patiently modeled forbearance, as when He had fed the five thousand and later suggested feeding the four thousand only to have the disciples question how it could be done.

Even in the Savior's own exhaustion, being awoken from sleep (how familiar does that sound?), He ultimately and patiently calmed His fearful disciples:

And he was in the hinder part of the ship, asleep on a pillow: and they awake him, and say unto him, Master, carest thou not that we perish? And he arose, and rebuked the wind, and said unto the sea, Peace, be still. And the wind ceased, and there was a great calm. (Mark 4:38–39)

He could have been angry or impatient or told them to solve the problem themselves.

Do we recognize the endless patience the Savior shows us? How often do we barely acknowledge His hand or presence in our lives, but when trials come upon us we plead fearfully, or tearfully, for relief? Then having received it, we go on our merry way, forgetting Him once again?

Perhaps just for today we can feel the Savior's patience in our lives.

How can you more fully thank Him for the patience He shows you?

DAY 18: HE FORGIVES

Luke 6:35–37

But love ye your enemies, and do good, and lend, hoping for nothing again; and your reward shall be great, and ye shall be the children of the Highest: for he is kind unto the unthankful and to the evil.

Be ye therefore merciful, as your Father also is merciful. Judge not, and ye shall not be judged: condemn not, and ye shall not be condemned: forgive, and ye shall be forgiven.

Recently I read the account of a man named Chris Williams and the drunk driver who killed Chris's wife and two children. At the same moment he realized his family members had died and that he wished to die himself, a voice filled his mind and said, "Let it go!" Then there came a power beyond his own helping him to feel peace, healing, and to understand what those commanding words meant. In the days and years ahead, the refrain of "Let it go!" returned often and continued to bring him peace.

Each of us likely has a good reason to not forgive someone—a horrible act, a hurtful phrase, a heartless response. And yet, as we let go we understand what the Savior is saying. He has already suffered the anguish, the hurt, and the sorrow for us in Gethsemane. When we hold on to negative feelings, we tie His hands and make it less possible for us to use the Atonement and to feel the peace, love, and joy it brings.

Just for today, forgive someone who has wronged you. Love someone you have turned away from. Be kind to someone who is unkind to you. Forgiveness is the key, and He is the one who provided it for us. We only need to use it.

How can you be more forgiving today?

DAY 19: HE IS CONFIDENT

Luke 2:46, 47

And it came to pass, that after three days they found him in the temple, sitting in the midst of the doctors, both hearing them, and asking them questions.

And all that heard him were astonished at his understanding and answers.

Even as a twelve-year-old boy, Jesus understood truth and could explain it better than the religious scholars of the day. That truth gave Him confidence and wisdom, which made Him able to converse in diverse situations and with various people, ranging from confused to murderous (as with the Pharisees).

When we are in a delicate situation or dealing with a difficult person, we can increase our confidence by knowing and living truth. No matter the rhetoric of the day, practicing principles as simple and sound as the Ten Commandments brings peace, joy, and a surety from within. These tenets work, though some try to change them. Jonathan Sacks, Britain's chief rabbi, lamented in a *Wall Street Journal* article that "The Ten Commandments [have been] rewritten as the Ten Creative Suggestions." (Quoted in Thomas S. Monson, "Stand in Holy Places," *Ensign*, October 2011.)

Although Jesus taught more than just the Ten Commandments, I'm continually amazed at how this concise set of divine directives has profoundly impacted so many lives:

Thou shalt have no other gods before me. Thou shalt not make unto thee any graven image. Thou shalt not take the name of the Lord thy God in vain. Remember the Sabbath day, to keep it holy. Honor thy father and thy mother. Thou shalt not kill. Thou shalt not commit adultery. Thou shalt not steal. Thou shalt not bear false witness. Thou shalt not covet. (See Exodus 20:2-17).

Following this basic creed produces a tangible moral confidence. This in turn positively influences people and encourages them to respect you, trust you, and help you succeed.

What basic commandment can you follow today to develop more core confidence?

DAY 20: HE IS TRUTH

Luke 8:49–55

While he yet spake, there cometh one from the ruler of the synagogue's house, saying to him,

Thy daughter is dead; trouble not the Master. But when Jesus heard it, he answered him, saying, Fear not: believe only, and she shall be made whole . . . And all wept, and bewailed her: but he said, Weep not; she is not dead, but sleepeth.

And they laughed him to scorn, knowing that she was dead. And he put them all out, and took her by the hand, and called, saying, Maid, arise. And her spirit came again, and she arose straightway.

This scripture story stays with me because of the people's response. Here is the Son of God, who has healed and accomplished miracles—repeatedly—and the people's response is to laugh at His assertion that the girl is only sleeping.

They basically say, "Don't you think we know a dead person when we see one?" Their perception obscures the truth. They are so sure of their own knowledge and experience that there can be no other outcome.

And yet there was. The Savior did the unbelievable, the miraculous, essentially only a few feet from them. And He did it gently, without throwing it in their faces or pointing a mocking finger back at them.

38

Sometimes we think we know all there is to know about situation, a person, or a story. And in our unwitting pride, we miss incredible opportunities and gifts. Assuming we know best robs us of loving others, of wiser perspectives, and of surprising friendships that we may not have anticipated.

Just when you think that all is lost, when hope falters, or when you think a situation—or person—will never, ever change, remember, He knows the truth. Because He is the Truth—the Way, and the Light—He can work miracles.

Turn your confusion over to Him and find out what you need to do to exercise greater faith and to foster a more open mindset to what is real and not perceived.

What is one situation you can see differently and more truthfully?

DAY 21: HE IS AWARE

Matthew 9:35–36

And Jesus went about all the cities and villages, teaching in their synagogues, and preaching the gospel of the kingdom, and healing every sickness and every disease among the people. But when he saw the multitudes, he was moved with compassion on them.

My daughter once shared a story about a little girl bringing her favorite treat to a classroom "trading day." Throughout the day's trading, she noticed a little boy with several small rocks on his desk and without any trading interest from others.

The little girl didn't want a rock but after a while could tell the boy was sad without having anyone take notice or want to participate with him. So she offered a treat for a rock and then surprised herself by asking if he also wanted to play basketball. He happily accepted both offers.

What I love about this child's story is her awareness. That is exactly how the Savior was and is—completely aware of each person and their particular needs, especially when they're not jumping up and down saying, "I'm here, pick me, pick me."

In our neighborhood lives a young adult woman who suffers from a mental illness and who has the mindset of young child. We wave or say hello whenever we see her. One day her mother approached me with a note and a smile. In the note she thanked me for my son Ethan's sweet attention to her daughter. She shared that Ethan made a special effort to say hello, talk with, and listen to her. When the young woman made a Valentine for my teenage son, he didn't balk at it or throw it away. Apparently, he had quietly made a kind note for her in return. I knew none of this. How grateful I was for his tender awareness and kindness.

Awareness seems to be the first step in compassion—the next being, of course, action. And as we become more aware and act, our lives and others' are blessed beyond measure.

How can you be more aware of, or more readily act on, the needs of someone else?

DAY 22: HE RESPECTS WOMEN

John 19:26–27

When Jesus therefore saw his mother, and the disciple standing by, whom he loved, he saith unto his mother, Woman, behold thy son!

Then saith he to the disciple, Behold thy mother! And from that hour that disciple took her unto his own home.

Repeatedly, we see the Savior's love and respect for women. In this moment of agony, the Savior looks down from the cross and sees His mother. With loving concern, He charges John, one of the Twelve, to now care for her.

To the young lady who brought ointment for His feet, He showed gratitude. Although others derided her actions, Jesus acknowledged her faith and good works, and forgave her sins.

And on the morning of the Resurrection, He notably first appeared to Mary Magdelene.

From the very beginning of His ministry, Jesus showed respect for women. At the wedding in Cana when the feast wine ran out, Jesus' mother mentions the fact and in essence suggests He can do something about it. Although Jesus replies it's not really His time yet to do such things, He performs His first miracle by turning water into wine. It's my understanding that He does this out of respect for His mother.

What a blessing good women are in our lives. Mothers, sister, friends, and neighbors—women so often and so well know how to nourish and nurture those around them. How often has a woman in your life nursed you back to health, remembered a birthday, sent you a sweet note, or given you a needed hug?

Jesus loved and respected all that a woman does and is, and showed this through His actions.

How can you express gratitude or show more respect for a woman in your life?

DAY 23: HE GENTLY CORRECTS

Luke 10:39-42

And she had a sister called Mary, which also sat at Jesus' feet, and heard his word. But Martha was cumbered about much serving, and came to him, and said, Lord, dost thou not care that my sister hath left me to serve alone? Bid her therefore that she help me.

And Jesus answered and said unto her, Martha, Martha, thou art careful and troubled about many things: But one thing is needful: and Mary hath chosen that good part, which shall not be taken away from her.

I'm probably one of the few who loves this passage because I see the Savior speaking gently with Martha, whom He loved. This good woman had a burning testimony of His divinity, and cared for Him often. Instead of getting angry or impatient or judging Martha, the Savior brought home what was happening to help her learn a principle.

Martha was showing her love by meeting the needs of the Savior and the people who gathered to hear Him. And yet what Martha needed most, as did Mary, was to listen and to feel the healing power of His words.

In this scripture, when the Savior says "careful," it can be translated to "worried." Are you worried about all there is to do? Are you "cumbered about much serving" and maybe even a bit resentful that you have so much to do and why can't someone else shoulder the burden or help you out?

Imagine the Savior speaking to you gently, looking into your eyes, and, with a loving smile, saying, "But one thing is needful." Then, reminding us to choose the good part. When we take time for needful things, when we prioritize our lives so that we are in tune with His will, we can peacefully approach our tasks and do so better knowing how to do them, enjoy them, and grow through them.

How can you deal more gently with others today?

DAY 24: HE COMFORTS

John 14:26

But the Comforter which is the Holy Ghost, whom the Father will send in my name, he shall teach you all things, and bring all things to your remembrance, whatsoever I have said unto you.

No matter who we are or what we're going through, the Savior can comfort us. While He was here on the earth, Jesus comforted in person. But He told the Apostles that after leaving them, He would then send the Second Comforter, the Holy Ghost, to bring warmth, truth, light, and peace. Even though Jesus would not physically be there, people could still feel His love.

After having our seventh child (at the age of forty-six!), I felt a tad overwhelmed with the new baby lifestyle, particularly sleep deprivation. One time our baby got the flu. Having already cared for other sick children, I was depleted before the baby's turn. At one point, my husband and I were up for three long, difficult nights without sleep and attempting to soothe a crying, inconsolable baby. By the third morning, I moved about the house, zombielike, feeling emotionally fragile and exhausted. When the baby began crying again, I just looked at my husband and I began to cry too.

My husband didn't say something perky or try to make it all better. He immediately walked over to me, embraced me as I almost collapsed in his arms, and we both knelt down on the floor. As I cried on his shoulder, he literally held and rocked me while our daughter cared for the baby. No words needed to be exchanged—I knew that he knew exactly how I felt, and in this moment, he stepped out of his similar need and gave me the comfort I needed.

That is the Savior—comforting, caring, and knowing exactly how and when to do so. He can, through the Comforter, give us that same feeling of being embraced and understood if we choose to let Him.

How can you let the Savior comfort you today?

DAY 25: HE RELATES TO OTHERS

Matthew 13:3, 10, 13

And he spake many things unto them in parables, saying, Behold a sower went forth to sow . . .

And the disciples came, and said unto him, Why speakest thou unto them in parables? . . .

[He said] because they seeing see not; and hearing they hear not, neither do they understand.

Using everyday items, Jesus taught about values and life lessons through simple but profound parables—stories, if you will. Candles and coins. Sheep and goats. Foolish rich men and reckless, prodigal sons. Things and situations the common people knew intimately. As the Savior spoke to these images, the people could better understand the parable, feel the message, and allow their hearts to be changed.

As we use this same method to relate to others in meaningful ways, we can change relationships.

One day as I drove my young teenage son to school, he went on and on about a favorite video game. Desiring him to be more spiritually minded, if only for a few minutes, I asked him to read from the scriptures. He said it would make him carsick to read in the car (though I had recently seen him read a Harry Potter book without becoming nauseated).

I said, "Okay. How about you tell me something spiritual about the video game?"

To my surprise and delight, he thought for a moment then began telling me that the red squares were like sin, and that the blue squares that gave extra coins were like repentance. Over the next few minutes, and without realizing it, he created a terrific parable about sin and repentance, one we still talk about to this day.

When talking with your children, giving a presentation, or comforting a friend, use familiar settings and language. Even if you don't like soccer or statistics or scrapbooking, consider how you can liken the situation to your listeners to make it more meaningful.

What is one way you can better relate to someone by using experiences or examples that are meaningful to them?

DAY 26: HE LOOKS ON PEOPLE'S HEARTS

Mark 12:42-44

And there came a certain poor widow, and she threw in two mites, which make a farthing.

And he called unto him his disciples, and saith unto them, Verily I say unto you, That this poor widow hath cast more in, than all they which have cast into the treasury:

For all they did cast in of their abundance; but she of her want did cast in all that she had, even all her living.

I marvel how, even in the busyness of the moment, Jesus noticed this poor woman. I marvel how He called the disciples and pointed out her actions to them, using the experience as a teaching opportunity. And I marvel how He commended her offering as a rightful sacrifice. The Savior was mindful of each and every person. No one was too poor, too unknown, too beneath His loving watchcare.

Time after time, interaction after interaction, we see the Savior get right to the heart of the matter. With the rich young man who asked how to get into heaven, He knew the one thing that would hold him back. Jesus rightfully told him to sell all he had and give it to the poor. With the woman at the well, He knew her receptivity and used the experience to teach gospel truths. With the woman taken in adultery, He knew the whole truth yet spoke clearly of the only thing that truly mattered—for her to go her way and change her life.

He knows you and me thoroughly. We are important to Him. In fact, we are His entire focus, even if we aren't well-known by the world, even if we don't have the perfect family or the loveliest home or the most spectacular accomplishments. Society judges our efforts and devotions by these measures, but He "looketh on the heart" and knows our sacrifices, our hopes and dreams, and our goodness.

What is one evidence in your life that Jesus knows you personally?

DAY 27: HE LIFTS BURDENS

Luke 4:40
Now when the sun was setting, all they that had any sick with divers diseases brought them unto him; and he laid his hands on every one of them, and healed them.

No matter the ailment—spiritual, physical, emotional, mental—the Lord healed those around Him who had the faith to be healed and who were willing to trust Him enough to lay their burdens at His feet. With His talents and abilities, He could have been or achieved anything, and to perfection, but He chose to spend His time serving even the most humble of followers.

Why spend time with the lowliest of society?

We find an answer in Mark 10:45: "For even the Son of man came not to be ministered unto, but to minister, and to give his life a ransom for many."

The Savior went about doing good to all, no matter a person's personality or status and independent of whether they'd been kind to Him or not. Throughout His ministry, He lifted burdens and made people whole.

What burdens do you need to release? What situations, experiences, or people's responses make you feel overwhelmed, frustrated, or seem beyond your capacity to bear? Whatever it is, He's felt it, lived it, and overcome it. But for Him to release us from those feelings, we must willingly and consciously lay those burdens at His feet—

through prayer, faith, and action—so that He can lift them as He knows best.

What is one burden you can release and give to the Savior?

DAY 28: HE UNDERSTANDS BETRAYAL

Luke 22:48

But Jesus said unto him, Judas, betrayest thou the Son of man with a kiss?

Whether it stems from a spouse, a friend, or a co-worker, most of us know how it feels to be betrayed. So does the Savior. Not only did He choose Judas as a disciple, but Jesus tutored, loved, and worked with Judas throughout His ministry.

And yet, even though Judas's choices basically set in motion the events leading to Jesus' death, the Savior doesn't spend extra time pointing the finger. Or rehearsing the betrayal. Or seeking revenge.

If you've been hurt by someone you love and respect, know that the Savior understands exactly how that feels. Especially when the person hasn't apologized, doesn't seem remorseful, or perhaps hasn't even acknowledged his or her part in the situation. From personal experience, Jesus knows how to comfort your heart, ease your pain, and heal the hurt as you come to forgive someone who has wronged you. It may take time. As someone once said, if we open our heart to forgiveness, when it comes, we'll be ready to give it. But however long it may be, Jesus stands ready to lift that painful burden as soon as you're ready to hand it over.

What past hurt or betrayal can I let go of today?

DAY 29: HE HELD DIFFICULT CONVERSATIONS

Mark 10:17, 18–22

And when he was gone forth into the way, there came one running, and kneeled to him, and asked him, Good Master, what shall I do that I may inherit eternal life?

Thou knowest the commandments, Do not commit adultery, Do not kill, Do not steal, Do not bear false witness, Defraud not, Honour thy father and mother. And he answered and said unto him, Master, all these have I observed from my youth.

Then Jesus beholding him loved him, and said unto him, One thing thou lackest: go thy way, sell whatsoever thou hast, and give to the poor, and thou shalt have treasure in heaven: and come, take up the cross, and follow me.

And he was sad at that saying, and went away grieved: for he had great possessions.

The Savior did not back down from uncomfortable situations. Instead, especially in this conversation, we see how He lovingly, carefully, and honestly speaks to the man before him.

In this passage we learn the key to successfully having difficult discussions: "Jesus beholding him loved him."

When you need to tell it straight, call someone on a comment, or address an emotionally-charged topic, begin with love for that person. When that good feeling threads your words, the person will feel it and know your intentions are good. And whether or not your words are accepted, he or she will know you care.

Years ago our family participated in a service auction. We bid on and bought a family night packet of visual aids and cookies made by a woman whose cookie-baking fame was neighborhood renowned. However, when the woman later brought the family packet it was without the cookies. I assumed she'd bring them later. When a few days passed, and without said cookies, I saw her at church and made a joking comment about the lack of refreshment.

She did not laugh.

At first, I let it go and realized that I was likely too focused on the cookies. But her expression stayed with me—not anger, more like exhaustion. The realization dawned on me that this good lady was the mother of several small children and had spent hours on making the visual aid kit. She likely had been too tired to even think about the cookies.

Instead of leaving that negativity between us, I took the opportunity to pull her aside. With candor and love, I apologized for my rudeness and listened to her personal story that confirmed my earlier conclusions. The easy rapport that had formerly existed between us returned.

How can you be more authentic in your conversations, especially difficult ones, today?

DAY 30: HE LOVES CHILDREN

Matthew 18:2–4
And Jesus called a little child unto him, and set him in the midst of them, And said, Verily I say unto you, Except ye be converted, and become as little children, ye shall not enter into the kingdom of heaven. Whosoever therefore shall humble himself as this little child, the same is greatest in the kingdom of heaven.

Jesus loves little children. I think it's incredible that the Son of God, in all His majesty and ability, was aware of and attentive to these smallest, and often considered the lowliest, of people. Maybe it was because they were innocent, humble, and teachable. Whatever the reason, I appreciate that He was their advocate, helping adults to value, learn from, and protect them.

In our society, I've seen a definite shift from family-friendly to barely family-tolerant. A few months ago the news told of a petition that had been started to ban babies from a certain grocery store (their noise was disturbing). My first thought was, did the people who drafted this petition not realize that *their* mothers had likely taken them to the store as babies?

In all that He did, Jesus showed that the greatest was the least and the least the greatest. We have seven children, and I learned long ago that parenting is not so much about teaching them all they need to know; it's being willing to learn all they're trying to teach me.

Through thick and thin, we love our children and feel privileged to be their parents. Years ago one of our children complained that there was a Mother's Day and a Father's Day but nothing for children—why was that?

We answered that excellent question by adopting a Japanese tradition and holding our own Children's Day (in July). Each year we do a fun family activity where we share why we love each child. Nothing major, just something to say you are special and appreciated.

What can you do today to more fully love, appreciate, or learn from a child?

DAY 31: HE TAKES TIME FOR PEOPLE

Luke 18: 35, 38-43

And it came to pass, that as he was come nigh unto Jericho, a certain blind man sat by the way side begging: And he cried, saying, Jesus, thou Son of David, have mercy on me.

And they which went before rebuked him, that he should hold his peace: but he cried so much the more, Thou Son of David, have mercy on me.

And Jesus stood, and commanded him to be brought unto him: and when he was come near, he asked him, Saying, What wilt thou that I shall do unto thee? And he said, Lord, that I may receive my sight. And Jesus said unto him, Receive thy sight: thy faith have saved thee. And immediately he received his sight.

I'm impressed with how the Savior takes time for this man. Jesus isn't hurrying down a list of errands or running to a meeting. Instead, He is sitting still and hears the cry for help. After hearing it, He doesn't ignore the man or schedule an appointment for later. Jesus simply stands, asks him to come close, and speaks with him. They converse and connect, and ultimately the man is healed.

How often are we running through our day, literally and figuratively, only to miss the people we could have influenced? Moving a little slower might make us more open to those who need our love and encouragement, and likely

60

won't interrupt the to-do list after all. I often find that when I remember to go about life more slowly and consciously, my to dos are either completed quicker or more conveniently.

At one point I was finishing a book with an imminent deadline. As usual, I typed only during my baby's nap time. But my baby caught the flu and for several days he was fussy, crying, and up all night. Day after day, I was inches from my laptop but unable to be productive. Then one morning it hit me—my son needed me, and that was the most important use of my time. *That* was being productive. Rather than be frustrated at the situation, I gave in freely to his needs. One particular day I did nothing but cuddle and feed him, both of us wrapped in warm blankets, going in and out of naps while the snow drifted outside.

What a keeper moment that was, and is. That's what mattered most—taking time to simply love and nurture my baby.

How can you spend more meaningful time with someone today?

DAY 32: HE COMPREHENDS MOTHERHOOD

Mark 6:54–56

And when they were come out of the ship, straightway they knew him . . . And ran through that whole region round about, and began to carry about in beds those that were sick, where they heard he was.

And whithersoever he entered, into villages, or cities, or country, they laid the sick in the streets, and besought him that they might touch if it were but the border of his garment: and as many as touched him were made whole.

Maybe it's because I'm knee deep in raising seven children, ages nineteen to seven months, but I can see in this scripture that Jesus understands exactly how it feels to be a mother.

The scripture says that the people came straightway—meaning, as soon as they caught sight of his ship they ran to Him like bees to honey. And then they ran and told everyone else to bring all *their* sick because look, He's here, and He will heal you!

Have you, to some degree, felt like that as a mother—that someone is always needing you or touching you, wanting to be made whole, or at least wanting to get their homework question answered or school paper signed? Busy helping, women often don't have time to go to the bathroom when they need to—a truth I can attest to from almost twenty years of mothering.

Jesus knew how it felt to have people throng Him for His healing power. Can you imagine the energy it took for Him to do that amount of healing? And yet you don't hear in the scriptures of someone coming up and saying, "Sit down, take a rest. I'll come back tomorrow." No, it seems everyone wanted what they wanted, when they wanted it, without considering how the Healer was doing.

Sometimes mothers feel like that—a little used and taken advantage of. The endless cooking, cleaning, washing, and carpooling feels expected rather than appreciated. So on those days when a spouse's gratitude seems scarce and society's expectations high, remember that He gets it. He knows how it feels, and He relied on His Father to help provide the energy to do it. So can we.

Just for today, appreciate how the Savior gave and served without price or complaint, and how He looked to spiritual renewal in order to achieve it.

What is one way the Savior's life is similar to my life as a mother?

DAY 33: HE UNDERSTANDS LONELINESS

Matthew 26:37-45

And he took with him Peter and the two sons of Zebedee, and began to be sorrowful and very heavy. Then saith he unto them, My soul is exceeding sorrowful, even unto death: tarry ye here, and watch with me . . . And he cometh unto the disciples, and findeth them asleep, and saith unto Peter, What, could ye not watch with me one hour?. . .

He went away again the second time, and prayed. . . And he came and found them asleep again: for their eyes were heavy. And he left them, and went away again, and prayed the third time, saying the same words.

Then cometh he to his disciples, and saith unto them, Sleep on now, and take your rest: behold, the hour is at hand, and the Son of man is betrayed into the hands of sinners.

After the constant tutoring, compassion, and love that the Savior had previously given these good disciples, in His hour of need, they weren't there for Him. While He suffered for the pain and sins of all mankind, His weary disciples slept.

Where was His solace and support? We know it ultimately came from heaven in the form of a ministering angel. But what about from his earthly companions?

I've thought a lot about that. We've all heard that leadership is lonely, and it can be, especially the more responsibility we bear. But loneliness comes to all of us at some point, especially in our cyber pseudo-connection world. We can have 652 likes on your social media and yet not have a friend to hug us on a bad day.

I remember reading about the late Princess Diana, how she would attend events where thousands of people thronged her. And then she would go home to an empty castle and a TV tray on her lap, watching television and eating alone.

If you've felt alone and without someone to share your life load, imagine being the Son of God. Who can understand what He felt or went through?

Only one—His Father.

The next time you feel alone, when you wonder if someone really cares about you, remember that He understands. Deeply. And that you can receive sure and complete companionship just as He did, by turning to your Heavenly Father and the Savior.

How can you more fully turn to God and feel of His daily companionship?

DAY 34: HE GIVES US TENDER MERCIES

Matthew 8:14–15

And when Jesus was come into Peter's house, he saw his wife's mother laid, and sick of a fever. And he touched her hand, and the fever left her: and she arose, and ministered unto them.

In the Savior's typical daily service to others, He became a remarkable tender mercy—a timely blessing—for countless people. One experience included the mother-in-law of one of the Lord's beloved Apostles. Jesus came to Peter's house, saw that Peter's mother-in-law was ill, and healed her. What a gift that He visited their home that day! I can imagine this elderly mother, perhaps sick for a few days and not getting better, strongly desiring to get up to finish her domestic tasks but too ill to move. How wonderful to be healed and able to move forward. What a blessing for that mother to have the Savior there at her time of need.

So many of these tender mercies abound in our lives. Do we recognize them as such?

One Christmas vacation our family took a trip to San Diego. We had planned to visit Sea World, and, from what we understood, it was cheaper to purchase the entrance tickets at the theme park. However, after arriving and noting the entrance fee, we realized it would cost almost one thousand dollars for our large family to attend this one event!

Inspired, we quickly got on our smartphones, found a

deal through the city, purchased *four* passes for the same amount as the one entrance fee, downloaded the information and quick response codes on our phone, and went right to the ticket lady who scanned them on-site. Within thirty minutes we were all having a marvelous time.

With six anxious and excited children in tow, *that* was a tender mercy.

After the trip, I asked each person to share their favorite experience. Then I felt impressed to ask how they could see the Lord making that experience happen. Suddenly the conversation moved from "That was so fun," to "It's amazing how that worked out."

Besides the cheaper tickets, we recounted smaller experiences that made a big difference, like our baby being amazingly sweet-tempered on the ten-hour car ride; the beach house, previously unseen, being perfect for our large family; being able to rent wet suits just minutes before the store closed on Christmas Eve (to boogie board on Christmas Day). Moment after moment, we realized how often blessings had been showered upon us to make that vacation a memorable one.

The Savior truly is in the details if we will only look for His hand. From a neighbor stopping by at the right time to finding the lost school report, His tender mercies abound in our lives.

What are some of the tender mercies the Lord has brought into your life?

DAY 35: HE ALLOWED OTHERS TO HELP HIM

Matthew 27:31–32

And after that they had mocked him, they took the robe off from him, and put his own raiment on him, and led him away to crucify him. And as they came out, they found a man of Cyrene, Simon by name: him they compelled to bear his cross.

Each time I read this, I envision the Savior walking along the stony path, bearing the crushing weight of the wooden cross. He has just experienced the spiritual, emotional, and physical horrors of Gethsemane, bleeding from every pore in suffering for every individual who has ever lived. And now He is making His way to Calvary's hill, bearing another burden. At one particular moment when His steps must have faltered, a man is asked to bear His cross.

And the Savior lets him.

In our go-go lives, so often I see people, particularly women, being so very brave and so very independent. Even when they need help or feel that they just can't go on, they find it difficult to let others help.

Just this once, ask. Even if you have to ask three times, or three people. Invite someone to share your load or help you carry it.

My mother just recently came to visit. In the middle of

my typical zoom-zoom doing, she said, "Let me help you." She had me take a nap, had the children clean their zones, and then did my laundry! When I awoke, I felt rested and renewed. It was a small but lovely thing. It's these moments that help us remember we're not to do this alone.

In what way can you ask someone to help you with your load?

DAY 36: HE BROUGHT HIS MOTHER JOY

Luke 2:52
And Jesus increased in wisdom and stature, and in favour with God and man.

I often think of how Mary must have loved her Son. How she must have joyed in watching Him grow and mature—in goodness and kindness, in wisdom and respect—as He prepared for His ministry.

Perhaps this resonates with me because, at times, my otherwise wonderful children seem determined to make me cry. Within a two-week period I had a child with three "think times" and *two* lunch detentions at school; another child recommended for a friendship-skills group because she had issues with another little girl; another with two very low grades and without any signs of hurrying to improve them; and another who not infrequently had sudden and *intense* hormonal fits about life and homework.

One night I started wailing to my husband. "Where have we gone wrong?"

After blowing my nose and receiving kind consolation from him—"It's them, not us"—we had a family powwow. We discussed our family's expectations, the power of good choices, and the consequences of poor ones. I shed a few tears—an effective way of dishing out the old mother-guilt—

and ended with quotes from a spiritual talk on achieving our potential and developing the positive and divine within us.

How much it sank in, I'm not sure.

However, the very next day I received two notes from teachers telling me wonderful things about my children. Then, while I was away at a doctor's appointment, the kids completed their deep-cleaning chores at home, apparently without fussing or "forgetting." And each child had done something to "make restitution" for their behavior: completing overdue homework, writing notes of apology to teachers and friends, and surmounting hormone swings while completing a difficult school paper.

In a possible Mary moment, I felt and expressed to them the absolute joy that comes from having obedient and respectful children.

Though our children do not have the Savior's divine calling, as parents we, like Mary, get to participate in the amazing process of their growth and maturation. And though some days—or weeks—may be forgettable at best, we can feel joy in our less-than-perfect children.

How can you find more joy in your children as they grow and learn?

DAY 37: HE JUDGES RIGHTEOUSLY

Luke 19:5–10

And when Jesus came to the place, he looked up, and saw him, and said unto him, Zacchæus, make haste, and come down; for today I must abide at thy house. And he made haste, and came down, and received him joyfully. And when they saw it, they all murmured, saying, That he was gone to be guest with a man that is a sinner.

And Zacchæus stood, and said unto the Lord; Behold, Lord, the half of my goods I give to the poor; and if I have taken any thing from any man by false accusation, I restore him fourfold.

And Jesus said unto him, This day is salvation come to this house. . . . For the Son of man is come to seek and to save that which was lost.

Repeatedly, I see how the Savior judged people righteously, not as society did.

Zacchaeus was the chief publican, the tax commissioner, as it were. In those days the corrupt Roman tax system allowed publicans to reap unethical wages off of the tax collections. But the Savior knew Zacchaeus's heart and asked to spend time with him, dining at his home. The encounter was so life changing for Zacchaeus that he gave away half of his goods.

We learn a similar lesson from the Savior when the centurion came to Him requesting that his servant be healed. The Savior responded immediately, asking to be taken to the servant. But the centurion knew of the local belief that it made a Jew unclean to be in the home of a Gentile. And so, as an officer accustomed to giving orders, he pointed out that he knew Jesus could but give the word and effect the healing. Jesus knew this centurion's heart and faith and rewarded both despite the crowd's reaction.

In these and other situations, the Savior sets an incredible and wonderful precedent for us. How often have we seen a woman at church, PTA, or the office who seemed put together, with beautiful and accomplished children, and a tidy and beautifully decorated home? Are we happy for her, or do we feel resentful and find fault? How often do we judge our neighbor by a rumor or a co-worker by his annoying habits? When we look beneath the exterior, we can see the heart, and dreams and abilities we may never have noticed. When we're willing to suspend unrighteous judgment, we're rewarded with a softness, appreciation, and connection we may not have expected.

How can you judge less and love more today?

DAY 38: HE CARES

John 11:32–35

Then when Mary was come where Jesus was, and saw him, she fell down at his feet, saying unto him, Lord, if thou hadst been here, my brother had not died.

When Jesus therefore saw her weeping, and the Jews also weeping which came with her, he groaned in the spirit, and was troubled, And said, Where have ye laid him? They said unto him, Lord, come and see.

Jesus wept.

Some tend to portray the Savior as stern, rebuking, and unmerciful. This couldn't be further from the truth. Jesus felt deeply and loved fully. Whether someone was hungry or blind, had leprosy or epileptic fits, Jesus healed and nurtured and cared for those who were willing to be. And not only were they healed and fed, their hearts and lives were changed forever, often freed from burdens emotional and physical. They were made whole.

Years ago when I had pneumonia, a woman in my neighborhood came over with a grocery bag full of movies and books. She had been dealing with a chronic illness for years and knew how it felt to be down, literally and figuratively.

Without knowing my tastes in entertainment, she boldly and intuitively shared my favorite types. I began reading for the first time the *At Home in Mitford* series, a delightful story of the comings and goings in a quaint community. The sweet series brought me joy, peace, and comfort. Not surprisingly, I finished the books and my bed-rest at the same time.

In the grand scheme of things, her simple gift may seem small. But for me, it was deeply healing and personally fulfilling to know someone cared enough to do something. Her personal comfort touched my heart. And it's reminded me to care like-wise when helping others during illness or discouraging times.

How can you boldly share of yourself today? Can you give a hug, forgiveness, a smile, a pot of soup? Share a little of yourself and you'll find two souls both healthier and happier.

What can you do to comfort or show compassion to someone today?

DAY 39: HE LOVES

John 20:11–16

But Mary stood without at the sepulchre weeping: and as she wept, she stooped down, and looked into the sepulchre . . . she turned herself back, and saw Jesus standing, and knew not that it was Jesus.

Jesus saith unto her, Woman, why weepest thou? whom seekest thou? She, supposing him to be the gardener, saith unto him, Sir, if thou have borne him hence, tell me where thou hast laid him, and I will take him away.

Jesus saith unto her, Mary. She turned herself, and saith unto him, Rabboni; which is to say, Master.

What a beautiful passage of scripture. The Savior had suffered in Gethsemane, and on Golgotha. Now came the miracle at the garden tomb. He had atoned for the sins of all mankind, had been crucified on the cross, and was laid to rest seemingly for the last time. And then, just as He had repeatedly told His disciples, He was resurrected.

It begs the question, why—why did He do these difficult, painful, incredible things?

Because He loves us.

He doesn't force that love on us; it is freely given. As I read scripture, I see how often it says "might" or "may"—that we *might* come to Him, that we *may* have more happiness. He has done every possible thing to make sure that we can be happy, joyful, and fulfilled.

And now it's our turn. We can choose to live life differently, to believe more fully, to understand more deeply His beautiful, functional, and life-giving gospel. To come to know, and love and follow Him more fully. To feel more peace, hope, and surety in this unsure world. And it's all there, just for us, if we're willing to receive it, because He loved us enough to make it possible.

How can you show more love for the Savior today?

DAY 40: HE LIVES!

Luke 24:6-8

He is not here, but is risen; remember how he spake unto you when he was yet in Galilee, Saying, The Son of man must be delivered into the hands of sinful men, and be crucified, and the third day rise again.

And they remembered his words.

Can you imagine the joy, and surprise, of the disciples at seeing their beloved Savior once again in the flesh? He had told them it would happen, had clearly said He would rise again on the third day. And though they had seen Jesus bring back the dead, their minds would not, perhaps could not, comprehend such a miracle.

And yet He ate, talked, and walked with them. They felt the prints of the nails in His hands and feet and knew, of a surety, that He lived again. And because of this, we will, too.

Is it any wonder that the celebration of this miraculous event occurs in the spring, when all of nature testifies of birth, growth, and renewal? The perennial flowers that bloom again announce that life continues, that death is not the end. Don't we experience a similar desire for renewal and growth? We feel a sudden urge to roll up our sleeves for spring cleaning, prepare for a spring trip, or dig into spring yard work. That desire to feel things coming back to life after a dormant winter permeates the entire spring season.

Likewise, I invite you to refresh your soul, and more fully live, by letting go of what holds you back, or renewing your will to face what's before you. As you let go or clean out or hand over those negative burdens, you will feel a spiritual and emotional renewal. You will feel hope. And an increase of joy. And those feelings will lead to love, with a desire to share more of yourself, and in turn allow yourself to receive more from others.

What is one way you can more fully live today?

BOOK CLUB QUESTIONS

1. What was your overall understanding of Jesus Christ before reading *40 Days with the Savior?* What new insights did you have about Jesus Christ after reading this book?

2. Which character traits of the Savior have resonated most with you?

3. How has trying to apply one of the Savior's traits influenced your own life?

4. What did you enjoy most about daily reading devotionals on the Savior?

5. Did your feelings or perceptions about reading scriptural text change after reading these devotionals?

6. Share one new behavior or response to a situation that you have learned. For example, although He only went about doing good, the Savior was judged unfairly throughout His ministry. Have been judged unfairly or misunderstood? What did you learn from it? How can you better respond in the future if it occurs again?

7. If you were to choose one character trait of the Savior you would like to possess right now, what would it be? Why?

8. What character traits of the Savior do you feel you have developed over the years? Which personal experiences helped you gain that growth?

9. After reading about the Savior's traits such as love, mercy, forgiveness, etc., which have you benefited most from in your life?

10. If you met the Savior today, what would you say to Him?

MY THOUGHTS

MY THOUGHTS

MY THOUGHTS

More Books From Connie Sokol

If you're not sure which to choose or where to begin, try the category you're most interested in.

Start a life change:
Faithful, Fit & Fabulous (faith-based)
Create a Powerful Life Plan

Inspirational:
40 Days with the Savior (faith-based)
Motherhood Matters (faith-based)
Faithful, Fit & Fabulous (faith-based)

Just for fun
The Life is Too Short Collection
Caribbean Crossroads (romance)

All titles are available as ebooks and print books at www.amazon.com or www.conniesokol.com.

Faithful, Fit & Fabulous: Get Back to Basics and Transform Your Life in 8 Weeks! (A simple life-planning, goal-setting system that helps moms tidy up 8 life areas in 8 weeks)

http://www.amazon.com/Faithful-Fit-Fabulous-Transform-ebook/dp/B005Z4CGDK/ref=sr_1_2?ie=UTF8&qid=1381964726&sr=8-2&keywords=connie+sokol

Create a Powerful Life Plan: 3 Simple Steps to Your Ideal Life (A step-by-step guide to creating a Life Plan that works)

http://www.amazon.com/Create-Powerful-Simple-Steps-ebook/dp/B00AY7P6M6/ref=sr_1_3?ie=UTF8&qid=1381964726&sr=8-3&keywords=connie+sokol

The Life is Too Short Collection—Kitchen Table Wisdom with a Side of Humor (A collection of the most-loved columns from the "Life Is Too Short" series)

http://www.amazon.com/Life-Too-Short-Collection-ebook/dp/B00C3976H6/ref=sr_1_4?ie=UTF8&qid=1381964726&sr=8-4&keywords=connie+sokol

Simplify & Savor the Season: Organize and Re-energize Your Holidays!

http://www.amazon.com/Simplify-Savor-Season-Organize-Re-energize/dp/0989019624/

Motherhood Matters: Joyful Reminders of the Divinity, Reality, and Rewards of Motherhood (A gift book)

http://www.amazon.com/Motherhood-Matters-Reminders-Divinity-ebook/dp/B007TY9HW2/ref=sr_1_7?ie=UTF8&qid=1381964726&sr=8-7&keywords=connie+sokol

Caribbean Crossroads (An award-nominated romance and #1 on Amazon Kindle)

http://www.amazon.com/Caribbean-Crossroads-Connie-E-Sokol-ebook/dp/B0089SWBTS/ref=sr_1_6?ie=UTF8&qid=1381964726&sr=8-6&keywords=connie+sokol

ACKNOWLEDGMENTS

My deepest appreciation to my women's church group for the original concept that I've now revised and personalized to create this, and the *24 Days with the Savior Christmas* e-books and booklets.

Abundant thanks to my editor, Michele Preisendorf; formatter Heather Justesen, cover artist Kelli Ann Morgan, and my gracious reviewers.

And finally, my heartfelt thanks to all those men and women who throughout the centuries have had a hand in preserving, teaching, and making the scriptures widely available for anyone who cares to read them.

I hope you enjoy this brief glimpse of the scriptures as much as I do.

Best,

Connie

ABOUT THE AUTHOR

Connie Sokol is a mother of seven, a sought-after national and local presenter, and a contributor on KSL TV's "Studio 5 with Brooke Walker" and "Motherhood Matters" blog. She is a former newspaper columnist, and TV and radio host. Mrs. Sokol is the author of several books including the award-nominated romance *Caribbean Crossroads, Faithful, Fit & Fabulous, The Life is Too Short Collection, Create a Powerful Life Plan,* and *Simplify & Savor the Season,* and, as well as talk CDs and podcasts. Mrs. Sokol marinates in time spent with her family and eating decadent treats. For her blog, video segments, products and more, visit www.conniesokol.com.